KEEPING
WATER CLEAN

Ewan McLeish

RAINTREE
STECK-VAUGHN
PUBLISHERS
The Steck-Vaughn Company

Austin, Texas

PROTECTING OUR PLANET

FORESTS FOR THE FUTURE

FUELS FOR THE FUTURE

KEEPING THE AIR CLEAN

KEEPING WATER CLEAN

PROTECTING WILD PLACES

WASTE, RECYCLING AND RE-USE

Published by Raintree Steck-Vaughn Publishers, an imprint of Steck-Vaughn Company

Library of Congress Cataloging-in-Publication Data
McLeish, Ewan.
Keeping water clean/ Ewan McLeish.
    p.   cm.—(Protecting our planet)
    Includes bibliographical references and index.
    ISBN 0-8172-4935-4
    1. Water quality management—Juvenile literature.
    2. Water—supply—Juvenile literature.
    I. Title. II. Series.
    TD365.M35 1998
    363.739'4—dc21   97-1257

Printed in Italy. Bound in the United States.
1 2 3 4 5 6 7 8 9 0 02 01 00 99 98

CONTENTS

INTRODUCTION

Water is the commonest substance on earth: it's almost everywhere. Even if you were living in the baking Australian desert, you would be able to find water somewhere—in the swollen underground part of a plant, perhaps, or the juicy body of a termite. In other parts of the world, people complain about getting too much water, as rain or snow. We even call it bad weather.

But we know that water is essential to life: without it we would die within a week. Even so, we take water for granted; we turn on a faucet and out it flows. It's a part of our everyday lives. Perhaps because of this we have not been very good at taking care of this valuable resource. And now, water is in danger.

In many developing countries, simple hand pumps like this bring clean water—and therefore life—to village people.

GOING, GOING, GONE?

- About 1.2 billion people—around a fifth of the world's population—do not have safe drinking water, and about 2 billion people in 80 countries live in areas with a chronic (continuous) shortage of water.
- Every day, more than 25,000 people die as a result of using unclean water.
- A 600-mi. (1,000-km) stretch of the Vistula River in Poland is so polluted with waste from factories and houses that its water cannot be used for anything.
- The "fallout" from air pollution caused by motor vehicles and industry is 1,000 times greater in the North Sea than in the South Pacific.
- Wealthy, developed countries such as the United States and Great Britain now have real water shortages—in many cases, for the first time ever.

THE SHRINKING SEA

The Aral Sea in Kazakhstan was once the fourth largest lake in the world. It supported a large fishing industry and was surrounded by fertile farmland producing large crops of cotton. But since the 1960s, the lake has been drying up. It is now only about half its original size, and by 2025 it may have disappeared altogether. Towns that were once busy fishing ports are now up to 40 mi. (60 km) from the lake shore.

The dry bed of the lake and the water that remains are severely contaminated by fertilizers and pesticides that were sprayed on the cotton crops, and this polluted soil is blown around by the wind and settles back on the fields. The fishing industry has collapsed. Illness has increased in the surrounding area, and one in ten babies die before they are a year old. The climate has begun to change: temperatures are becoming more extreme and there is less rain.

All these complex problems have one, simple cause. The Aral Sea is drying up because too much water is being taken out of it to irrigate the cotton.

Why have things become so bad? How can we have been so careless with our water supplies? To answer these questions, we first have to understand about water itself.

▲ These dead fish are the result of pollution of part of the Seine River, in France.

◀ These floating booms were used to try to prevent oil from escaping after the giant oil tanker *Exxon Valdez* ran aground in Prince William Sound, Alaska, in 1989. Huge areas of coastline were damaged by the spill.

WATER—NATURALLY

Water is common. However, 97 percent of all water that exists on our planet is seawater and therefore undrinkable. The remaining 3 percent is freshwater but most of this—nearly four-fifths—is locked in the ice caps and glaciers of the polar regions. Another one-fifth lies deep underground, and some exists as water vapor in the atmosphere. Only about 1 percent of all the world's freshwater is in lakes and rivers and in the soil. This 1 percent has to sustain all life on Earth, and by polluting it and wasting it we are putting ourselves—and other living things—in great danger.

DISTRIBUTION OF THE WORLD'S WATER

All Water

OCEANS 97%

FRESHWATER 3%

Freshwater

ICE CAPS & GLACIERS 79%

EASILY ACCESSIBLE SURFACE FRESHWATER 1%

GROUNDWATER 20%

Easily accessible surface freshwater

LAKES 52%

WATER WITHIN LIVING ORGANISMS 1%

SOIL MOISTURE 38%

RIVERS 1%

ATMOSPHERIC WATER VAPOR 8%

▲ How the world's water is distributed

▶ Lake Baikal—the world's deepest lake. Because it is so isolated, many types of animals are found there and nowhere else; it even has a unique freshwater seal named after it.

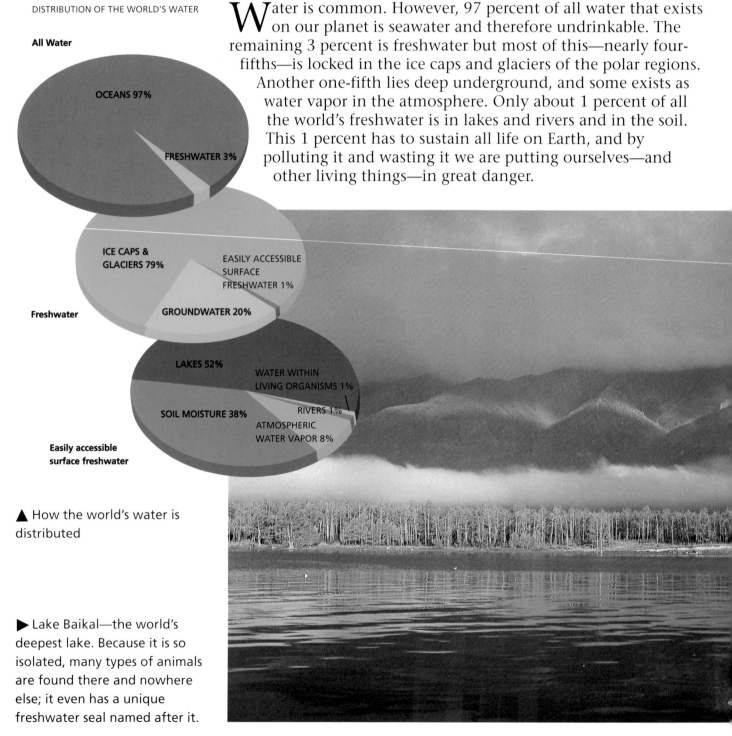

THE WORLD'S BIGGEST CYCLE

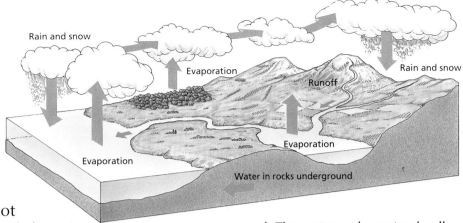

All the water in rivers and streams eventually ends up in the sea, but it doesn't stay there. Water is constantly evaporating—that is, escaping into the atmosphere as a gas or water vapor. The rate at which it evaporates increases with temperature. Evaporation occurs not only from the sea, but also from land, from rivers and lakes, and even from plants and animals. Once in the atmosphere, water vapor can travel long distances before it cools and condenses, forming clouds of water droplets. The droplets increase in size until they are too heavy to be held in the clouds and fall as rain or snow. This may fall directly back into the sea, but much of it falls on land to top off the lakes and rivers and the soil. It is this great water pump—the water or hydrological cycle—that makes life on Earth possible.

▲ The water cycle: water, in all its forms, is never stationary but always on the move. Without the water cycle to replace supplies, nothing on land could survive.

Pollution can enter the system at many stages in the water cycle. By polluting the air, we also pollute the water droplets it carries. When we pollute the land, rainwater can wash the pollutants into rivers and seas. And when we dump waste into the seas, we risk poisoning a vast range of habitats—and a source of food for many millions of people.

WATER RECORD-BREAKERS

- The largest ocean in the world is the Pacific. It makes up nearly half of all the world's oceans and covers almost a third of the earth's surface. Its average depth is 12,923 ft. (3,939 m).
- The largest freshwater (nonsalty) lake in the world is Lake Superior in North America; it covers an area twice the size of Denmark. But the lake containing the most water is Lake Baikal in Siberia.

Lake Baikal contains about 20 percent of all the world's freshwater. At 5,315 ft. (1,620 m) it's also the deepest.
- The world's longest river is the Nile in Africa, at 4,000 mi. (6,437 km), but the river with the greatest flow is the Amazon in South America. More water flows from the mouth of the Amazon than from the next ten biggest rivers put together.

WATER FOR LIFE

Every living thing needs water in some form. Some seeds and spores (the seedlike parts of fungi and mosses) can survive for hundreds of years in a completely dry state, but they still need water before they can germinate and grow.

Our own bodies are actually about two-thirds water. This doesn't mean it's sloshing around inside us. All living things are made of cells, and cells are mainly water. Some parts of the body, such as bone, contain very little water; other parts, like the blood, are about 90 percent water. Everything that goes on in the body—such as digestion, keeping cool, breathing, and getting rid of waste—needs water. If we become dehydrated and lose more than 15 percent of our body water, we die.

TOADS IN THE DESERT

The spadefoot toad lives in the waterless Arizona desert, where it spends years buried in the dry mud. Then, as soon as it rains, the toads emerge from their underground chambers. The females lay eggs and, in a day or two, tadpoles are jostling in the muddy pools. Within a few days, the tadpoles develop into adult toads. As the pools dry out, the toads bury themselves again. They remain underground until it rains again in a few years.

A spadefoot toad burrows into the mud of the Arizona desert after the rains. Soon the mud will be baked hard. The toad will not emerge again until the rains return.

STANDING UP FOR THEMSELVES

Plants are just as dependent on water as are animals. Tomatoes and cucumbers are about 95 percent water. Besides being necessary for chemical reactions and for transporting dissolved substances through the plant, water pressure in plant cells provides a sort of liquid skeleton that enables plants to remain rigid. Everyone has seen plants drooping or wilting in hot weather. It is a sign that water is being lost more quickly by evaporation from the leaves than it is being replaced through the roots. Giving the plant some water will make it look much healthier.

A FRAGILE RESOURCE

While all living things need water to survive, not just any old water will do. If water is polluted with harmful chemicals or dangerous bacteria, it can damage and destroy life rather than supporting it. For example, when an oil tanker spills its cargo into the sea, huge numbers of marine animals and seabirds can be killed by the oil. Industrial chemicals released into a river can poison all the fish a long way downstream. And drinking unclean water causes the deaths of millions of people every year.

The water from this waste pipe has been polluted by human activity. We have to balance the benefits we get from industry against the damage such activities can do to the environment.

LIVING IN WATER

Animals and plants live in the sea and in freshwater (rivers, lakes, and ponds). Water, especially seawater, is ideal for supporting life. In proportion to its size, a coral reef contains more living things than a tropical forest. The vast swarms of plankton—tiny plants and animals—that float in the sea produce more food than all the vast grasslands of Africa and South America.

LIFE BENEATH THE WAVES

The sea is not one habitat but actually many. In the open ocean, almost all animals depend on microscopic floating plants, called phytoplankton, that live in the well-lit upper waters, down to a depth of about 650 ft. (200 m). These form food for tiny animals called zooplankton that, in turn, are eaten by small fish. These small fish form the main diet of larger fish and other hunters, like squid. At the top of this food chain are the big predators—sharks, tuna, and mammals such as killer whales, seals, and dolphins.

LIVING IN FRESHWATER

Rivers, lakes, and ponds are very different places to live in than the sea. Most rivers start as small streams, often high in the hills. Here the water is usually cold, clear, and fast flowing, with plenty of oxygen but few dissolved nutrients to support plant life.

Clean water can support an enormous variety of life—including humans. Here two lion fish and a school of glass fish surround a diver in the crystal-clear water.

As more streams join a river, it becomes wider and slower. It carries a load of fine mud or silt washed from the banks and the riverbed. The water is richer in nutrients but contains less oxygen.

In its final stages, a river is broad and winds over a wide, flat plain that may flood after heavy rain. As it reaches the sea, a river may become even wider or divide many times as it flows across a delta.

Freshwater habitats are normally much smaller than seas and oceans, so their temperature and water level can change rapidly. They are also more easily affected by substances that flow into them from the surrounding land. Where the land is farmed intensively or there are towns or industry nearby, these substances can be harmful. In November 1986, 30 tons of highly poisonous chemicals washed into the Rhine River in Switzerland. Within 10 days, everything in the river was killed for more than 185 mi. (300 km) downstream.

▲ The stages of a river: as the river widens, it becomes slower and is more easily affected by substances washed in from the land, including chemicals that can pollute the water.

◄ A typical food chain or food web in the sea; each organism can be eaten by the next one in the chain.

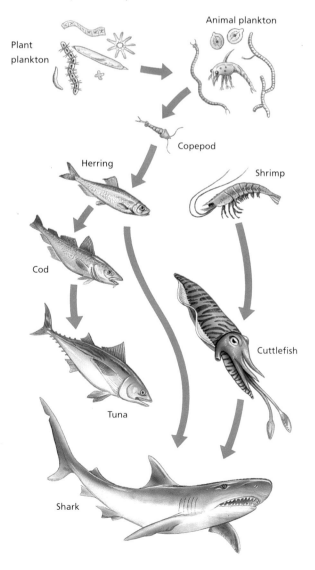

PASS IT ON...

Even though they are vast, the oceans—and the life they support—can be severely affected by pollutants that flow into them from rivers or are dumped in them from ships. When organisms at the bottom of the food chain, such as plankton, take in poisonous chemicals from pollution, they pass them on to the fish that eat them, and so on. In this way, the poisons pass up the food chain. But that isn't all: the poisons also become more and more concentrated as they move up the chain. So although a small fish may not take in a fatal amount of poison, by the time a dolphin has eaten lots of large fish, which have all eaten lots of small fish, the poison may be strong enough to kill the dolphin.

WATER IN THE WORLD

Water doesn't stay in the same place: it's constantly in motion, in lakes and rivers, in the atmosphere, and in the sea. It is moved by some of the most powerful forces on earth.

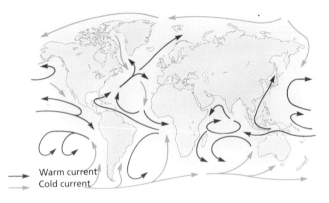

Warm current
Cold current

▲ The world's ocean currents

RIVERS IN THE SEA
When you visit the coast, you may see signs warning of dangerous currents in the sea. These are usually local currents caused by the tides. But in the deep oceans there are much greater currents, like enormously wide rivers, which move unimaginable volumes of water across the face of the earth.

These currents are produced by a combination of winds, called prevailing winds, that blow in a constant direction, and the rotation of the earth in space. The effect is to produce enormous circular flows of water in all the main oceans. The Gulf Stream moves warm water from the Gulf of Mexico up the eastern coast of the United States and across the North Atlantic Ocean to northern Europe. Currents like these affect the types of animals and plants found in the sea. Some creatures, like the leatherback turtle, even use them to hitch rides across the oceans.

▶ Pollution from the land has caused tiny marine plants called algae to grow in such numbers that they color the sea; fish and other animals swimming into this area may be killed by poisonous substances produced by the algae.

DANGEROUS CARGOES

Currents not only transport warm and cold water around the world: they also carry substances that are dissolved or floating in the water. Every year thousands of tons of garbage that has been dumped from ships in midocean ends up on beaches worldwide. Oil that is lost from oil tankers in major shipping lanes is spread rapidly over the surface of the sea by wind and currents. Even chemicals dumped in barrels on the deep seabed may not be safe forever. As the barrels slowly rust, underwater currents may eventually return the leaking chemicals to shallow seas and beaches.

▶ A sewage outflow on a beach in the Italian Riviera. With an average of 72 hotels for each mile (45 for each km) of coastline, the disposal of human waste has become a major pollution problem.

TIME AND TIDE

On almost every coast throughout the world, the sea level rises and falls twice a day. The gravitational pull of the moon and the sun drags the sea backward and forward as the earth rotates, causing tides.

The tides are often responsible for washing human waste back to the shore, even when it has been piped several miles (kilometers) out to sea.

Lakes also have tides, although they are usually too small to notice. Here the main danger comes from changing water levels. As the water level drops during the summer, or when water is taken out to replenish the water supply, a "dead zone" is created where few animals or plants can survive.

WATER AND PEOPLE

In the developed countries, such as those in Europe and North America, water comes from several sources. Its collection, purification, and distribution usually involve high cost, highly sophisticated technology, and large-scale engineering. Private water companies or government-owned water authorities are responsible for most water supplies.

FINDING WATER

- In upland areas, rain falling on hillsides rapidly collects into streams and rivers. These streams flow into valleys, which can be turned into lakes or reservoirs by building dams.
- In lowland areas, water is often taken directly from rivers and is pumped either straight to treatment plants for purification or into nearby storage reservoirs to be used later.

▲ This river valley has been dammed to create a reservoir. Reservoirs provide not only water but also opportunities for leisure. But dams may also flood land used by a wide variety of animals.

- Water collects in water-bearing (porous) rock—such as chalk, limestone, and sandstone—and forms aquifers. The water is then pumped out from wells or boreholes drilled down into the aquifer. Sometimes underground water supplies are "topped off" artificially from rivers or other water sources, a process known as recharging.
- An aquifer usually lies on top of nonporous rock. If the two layers of rock reach the surface on the side of a hill, springs may occur. Since the water that flows from a spring has already been filtered through rock, it is usually very pure and can often be bottled and sold as natural spring water.

▼ The shape and composition of these rocks creates the perfect conditions for an aquifer. The water trapped in the porous rock can be reached by a borehole.

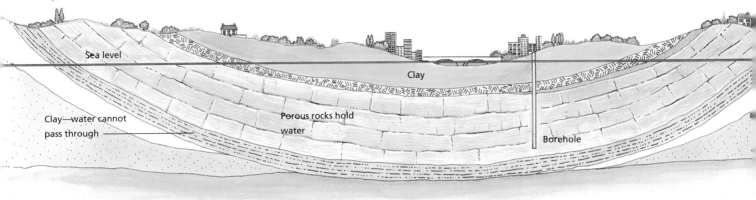

Sea level

Clay

Clay—water cannot pass through

Porous rocks hold water

Borehole

14

MAKING IT PURE

Most of our water supplies have to be purified before they reach our faucets. First, large bits of garbage, such as twigs, are removed, and the water is then treated with ozone to kill bacteria. Next, a chemical is added that makes any remaining particles, dead bacteria, and so on, stick together so they can be removed. The water is filtered through sand and then through carbon to get rid of any tastes and smells. Finally, it is treated with chlorine to kill any remaining bacteria, and then it's ready to drink.

IN THE PIPELINE

After purification, water is pumped through a network of pipes or water mains. These vary from 10 ft. (3 m) wide to less than 2 in. (3 cm), depending on where they are in the network. Most modern pipes are made of plastic since these are less likely to burst than the older metal pipes. A big city has more than a thousand miles (several thousand kilometers) of water mains, all buried underground. Locating and fixing a burst water main is no joke.

▶ Stages in the treatment and supply of drinking water in most developed countries

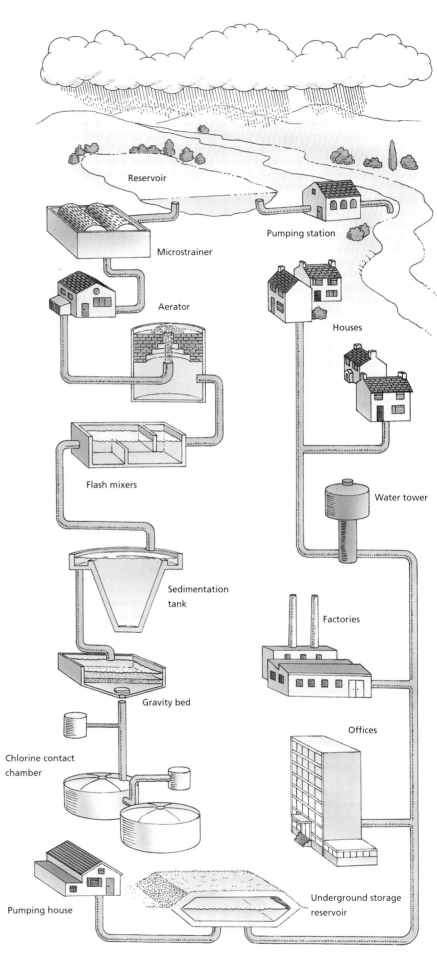

Reservoir

Pumping station

Microstrainer

Aerator

Houses

Flash mixers

Water tower

Sedimentation tank

Factories

Gravity bed

Offices

Chlorine contact chamber

Pumping house

Underground storage reservoir

WATER IN THE DEVELOPING WORLD

For many of the world's developing countries, such as those in parts of Africa and Asia, water is a scarce and precious commodity. Outside the richer parts of cities, water is rarely supplied in pipes. Usually people have to carry it themselves. In rural areas this often means a long walk to a river, pond, or spring, where the water is frequently dirty and unsafe. More fortunate areas have wells, but even these have their problems.

THE TROUBLE WITH WELLS

Wells make use of underground water that, like spring water, is naturally purified as it filters down through the soil and rock. But because the sides of traditional wells are not usually lined or the top covered, the water is easily polluted.

▲ Digging a well in Cambodia, Southeast Asia. The well has already reached the water table, so water has to be pumped out continuously to enable the workers to continue digging.

WELL FACTS

● Most hand-dug wells are 4.25 ft. (1.3 m) in diameter—the smallest size needed for two people to work inside. Two people dig more in one day than one person can in two days.

● Tube wells are the quickest wells to dig. They are bored out using a hand-operated auger—a type of giant drill turned by several people. Five people can drill up to 100 ft. (30 m) a day if the rock is not too hard.

● The amount of water underground decreases during the dry season as water is removed. Wells therefore have to be deep enough to reach below the water table—the level of water in the ground—at the driest time of year.

AN IMPORTANT PERSON

Khoki Rani is an important member of her community in the village of Golabaria, Bangladesh. She is trained as the village pump caretaker and can strip down and repair a hand-pump quicker than most people can change a faucet washer. "I was given a week's training in maintenance of the tube well. I do small repairs, and being a caretaker is accepted by all the village— even the men," she jokes.

▲ Khoki Rani—village pump caretaker and ace mechanic

Wells are often surrounded by pools of stagnant water, which provide breeding grounds for disease-carrying insects. More modern wells are usually lined with concrete and have lids. The area around the well is often drained to prevent stagnant water from collecting.

ALL DONE BY GRAVITY

Wells are not the only way of getting water. In hilly areas, water can be piped down to villages from streams higher up the valley. Water supplied by gravity does not need a pump, so less maintenance is required. But the pipes have to be taken care of and the water kept clean.

17

WATER UNDER THREAT

A person in one of the developed countries uses, on average, about 40 gal. (150 l) of water a day for washing, cooking, flushing the toilet, cleaning the car, and watering the garden. In poorer, dryer countries, it may be only 10 percent or even 5 percent of that amount.

HOW MUCH IS THAT?

It can be hard to picture that quantity of water. Try imagining 450 soft drink cans. If you were made entirely of water, then 40 gal. (150 l) of water would be enough to make about three of you.

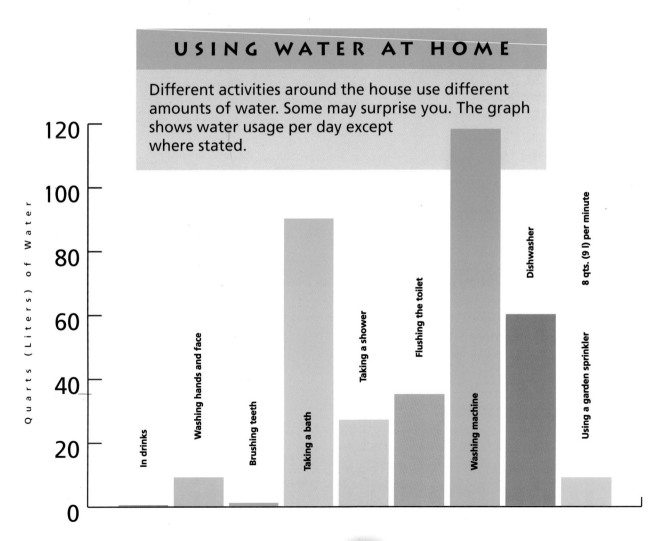

USING WATER AT HOME

Different activities around the house use different amounts of water. Some may surprise you. The graph shows water usage per day except where stated.

Quarts (Liters) of Water

120
100
80
60
40
20
0

In drinks
Washing hands and face
Brushing teeth
Taking a bath
Taking a shower
Flushing the toilet
Washing machine
Dishwasher
Using a garden sprinkler
8 qts. (9 l) per minute

As we have already seen, almost everything that we buy, use, eat, and drink uses or contains water. In fact, we use far more water in factories, farming, power stations, and other industries than we do at home. If you add this to our personal use, daily consumption shoots up to over 264 gal. (1,000 l)—that's a ton of water a day for each person.

WATER WORKING FOR US

To produce each of the following, we use about:

Product	Water Required
A car	119,000 gal. (450,000 l)
A ton of synthetic material (e.g., nylon)	37,000 gal. (140,000 l)
A ton of paper	14,300 gal. (54,000 l)
A bag of cement	48 gal. (180 l)
A bicycle	34 gal. (130 l)
A pair of shoes	14 gal. (53 l)
A Sunday newspaper	5 gal. (20 l)
A bar of chocolate	1 qt. (1 l)
This page	18 oz. (0.5 l)

▲ A power station in Navajo, Arizona. The white emissions are not smoke but steam caused by the evaporation of thousands of gallons of water used for cooling.

▼ Paper mills produce large quantities of dirty or wastewater. This mill in Finland has its own treatment works to clean up the water before it is allowed to leave the site.

The water it takes to produce a car would fill quite a large swimming pool.

DOING MORE WITH LESS

Of course, it's possible to live using a lot less water than we do. Where water is scarce, people regularly get by on less than 5.5 gal. (20 l) or often less than half that. That isn't necessarily a good thing, but it does say a lot about the huge quantities of water we use in developed countries.

Part of the huge sewage plant near London, England, which treats the wastewater produced by 2 million people.

CLEANING UP

Every time we use water it has to be cleaned in some way. Of course, some things make it dirtier than others. Water used for cooling in power stations becomes warmer but not really dirtier. Water that comes from toilets or from a paper-making factory needs much more treatment to make it clean again.

In developed countries, most used water ends up down a sewer, and most sewers lead to sewage or treatment plants. Treatment plants are amazing places: they turn water that is full of sewage into water that can be returned to rivers and the sea, and so rejoin the water cycle. And it's all—or nearly all—done with microbes.

GETTING THE TREATMENT

● On arrival at the treatment plant, sewage or wastewater is screened using large metal grids to strain out large objects such as wood, cans, and plastics.

● Next, the wastewater flows along deep, wide channels where gravel and sand sink to the bottom.

● The water is then pumped into large sedimentation tanks. Here solid particles sink to the bottom to form a thick sludge.

● The "settled sewage" (dirty water) is sprinkled onto large circular beds, about 6 ft. (2 m) deep, filled with stones. Millions of bacteria and other minute organisms living on the surface of the stones break down the remaining waste material, changing it to carbon dioxide, water, and simple nitrogen-containing compounds. This is called biological filtration.

● Instead of biological filtration, sludge already containing bacteria—known as activated sludge—can be fed into tanks of settled sewage along with large amounts of air. The bacteria multiply rapidly in these conditions, breaking down the waste.

● The treated water enters a final settling tank allowing any remaining particles to settle out before the cleaned water is returned to rivers and streams.

DOES IT WORK?

In theory, the way in which water is cleaned and treated sounds fine, but it doesn't always happen as it is described earlier. Even in developed countries, not all sewage is treated. In areas near the coast, some is still pumped—only partly treated or not treated at all, directly into the sea. This occurs especially in the summer when many people visit the coast and treatment systems become overloaded. At other times of the year, flooding may cause sewers to overflow and contaminate rivers and water supplies.

Some treatment plants are unable to deal with very high levels of phosphates from dishwashing liquids and detergents. Others do not work as efficiently as they should, particularly if they have been operating for some time and the filter beds have become clogged.

◀ In the Northwest Territories, in Canada, sewage disposal can be a real problem because in the cold climate the waste is very slow to break down. Here sewage from an Arctic village is pumped into a storage lagoon.

WHAT ABOUT THE SLUDGE?

Sludge from the treatment process is rich in nutrients such as nitrogen and phosphorus, which all plants need in order to grow. Much of it ends up as fertilizer on farmers' fields. But sludge from industrial areas may also contain high levels of poisonous or toxic metals such as mercury, copper, and cadmium. This is usually buried in landfill sites or burned.

▶ Sewage sludge is used as a liquid fertilizer on this farm in Anklam, Germany.

NATURE'S OWN SEWAGE TREATMENT!

Another approach to sewage is to let more natural methods take over. Reedbeds are excellent for treating wastewater. Because they often grow in mud where there is little oxygen, they absorb it through their leaves. The oxygen is pumped down to the roots, where it helps bacteria in the mud break down human and even industrial waste. Reedbeds could be the sewage treatment plants of the future. Several towns in Germany and a factory in Wales now treat their sewage in this way, and in parts of India reedbeds have been used for years.

In many developing countries, only the rich have access to proper sanitation. Around the outskirts of many cities, sewers are open drains. Here children play near an open sewer in Guatemala City.

PROS AND CONS

In recent years, there has been concern about the level of some human hormones found in water supplies even after treatment. Some people believe that this is due to increases in the use of oral contraceptives ("the pill"). However, another suggestion is that the water treatment process itself in some way activates hormones that are already present in the water in an inactive state. Whatever the case, it is important to understand that any system will have advantages and disadvantages. There is no perfect or right way of doing things.

USING RESOURCES WISELY

In developing countries, sewers and treatment plants are mainly for the benefit of the rich or those living in cities. Most toilets (or latrines as they are often called) are simple pits, covered with a concrete slab. Flushing may simply be a case of pouring in water by hand. In dry regions, however, even this can be a luxury.

Perfectly hygienic toilets can be designed that use little or no water at all (see box below). The most common type is the dry pit, which is a lined hole dug beneath a small cubicle. Although these types of latrines may sound a bit primitive, it's important not to jump to conclusions. These methods of disposal do not differ that widely, in principle, from the more "advanced" water-based systems described on page 22. They are also a lot cheaper. Furthermore, they represent a sensible use of the resources that are available. "Simple" does not always mean "not as good."

In these purification ponds in southern Thailand, wastewater from food processing is treated with bacteria and algae until it is clean enough to be returned to neighboring lakes.

WATER-FREE TOILETS

In developing countries, even in cities, many poor people have no access to sanitation, and their streets are open sewers. In the countryside the problem is less obvious but just as important for health. Well-designed, water-free toilets can help.

The simplest solution—digging a hole and making a concrete stand for your feet—is smelly and unhealthy. The British charity WaterAid has been encouraging villagers to build a better type of toilet (called a VIP latrine) that is designed to get rid of smells and keep out flies and other insects. It consists of a small cubicle built over a dry pit at least 10 ft. (3 m) deep. Smells and insects are removed from the pit by warm air rising through a vent pipe. No water is used in the latrine, but it is important that people wash their hands after using it. If they do that, the VIP latrine can be just as healthy as a flushing toilet.

In time the pit fills up. The latrine is then moved to a new pit, and the old pit is covered. After another three years, the old pit can be dug out and the contents used on the land as fertilizer.

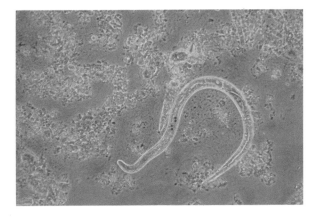

▲ Microscopic killers? A sample of sewage water under high magnification shows the minute organisms that inhabit dirty water.

▼ Cycle of death: how the schistosome worm infects people. Only by improving sanitation and preventing sewage from getting into water supplies can diseases like this be prevented.

A MATTER OF LIFE AND DEATH

In many parts of the world, poor wastewater disposal means that used water gets back into water supplies without being properly treated. The result is water-borne disease. Every day 25,000 people, most of them children, die from using unclean water. Dirty water is the world's single greatest killer. Most people have had diarrhea. It is inconvenient and uncomfortable, but it isn't usually dangerous—at least in developed countries. Yet, throughout the world, diarrhea caused by contact with unclean water kills 4 million young children every year. It kills because children lose too much liquid, sugar, and salt from the body. And even if it doesn't kill, constant illness slows growth and stunts mental development.

IT GETS UNDER YOUR SKIN

There is another disease of unclean water. It is called schistosomiasis and it is caused by a tiny parasitic worm that lives for part of its life in water snails. Then it leaves the snail and swims freely in the water. If a person enters the water, the worm burrows through the skin and ends up in the veins around the intestine.

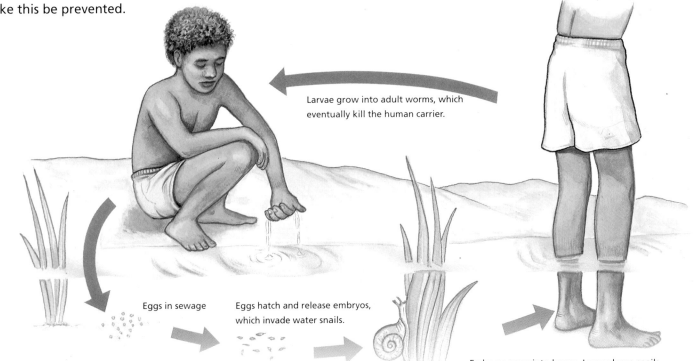

Larvae grow into adult worms, which eventually kill the human carrier.

Eggs in sewage

Eggs hatch and release embryos, which invade water snails.

Embryos grow into larvae. Larvae leave snails, penetrate human skin, and enter blood.

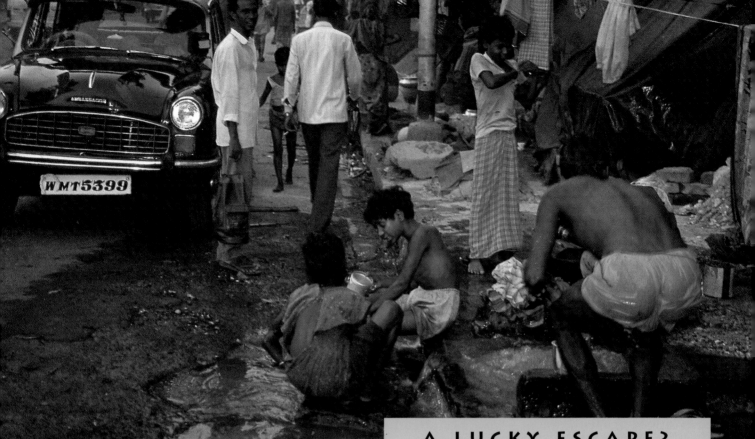

▲ For many, running water is a luxury. Here poor people in Calcutta, India, have to collect water from the street. It is unlikely the water is clean.

Here it produces millions of eggs that find their way into the intestine itself and leave the body when the person goes to the toilet. If the wastewater is not cleaned properly, the eggs may get back into the water in rivers and lakes. They hatch, find another snail, and the cycle is complete. Meanwhile, back in the bloodstream, the parasite is busy damaging the intestine, the lungs, and the liver. People become too sick to work or to resist other illnesses. Then they

BREAKING THE CYCLE

About 200 million people worldwide suffer from schistosomias Around Lake Volta in Ghana, nearly every child has it. Another 500 million suffer from trachoma, an eye disease that causes great pain every time they blink, followed by blindness. Other serious diseases, such as hookworm and roundworm, affect millions more. These diseases are all caused by unclean water.

The answer to the problem of water-borne disease seems obvious—clean water for all and proper disposal of human waste away from water supplies. But carrying that out is far from simple.

A LUCKY ESCAPE?

"Three months ago my children were very ill with diarrhea. We are lucky that a hospital is close to the village, so my husband and I carried them there. Before the health education classes, we thought the hot weather caused the illness, but now we know that it is due to bad water."
Putali Devi Tripathi—Nepal

▼ Putali Devi Tripathi: because of better education, Putali now understands the importance of clean water.

25

▲ This pond in France has been covered by a thick layer of algae due to organic pollution. Very little can survive in these conditions.

WHEN POLLUTION OCCURS

Most waste will break down naturally in water or in treatment plants. But sometimes there is just too much waste—or waste of the wrong kind. Then pollution occurs.

SUFFOCATING IN WATER

Pollution works in different ways. When organic waste, such as sewage or animal waste from farms, gets into water, bacteria begin to break it down in exactly the same way as in a treatment plant. But this process requires oxygen. As a result, oxygen is rapidly removed from the water, and animals and plants start to die.

Farm fertilizers can have similar effects. If they are washed into rivers or streams, they cause simple plants called algae to grow rapidly in the water. The algae cover the surface or make the water so cloudy that light is blocked from other water plants. Then the algae die, bacteria break them down, oxygen is removed from the water, and plants and animals die.

POLLUTING POWER

Different substances have different amounts of "polluting power," depending on how much oxygen is needed to break them down. If reasonably clean river water has a polluting power of 1 unit, then ordinary sewage would be 4 units (it would need four times as much oxygen to break it down). Waste from a pig farm would be 20 units and "liquor" escaping from stored hay (silage) would be 45 units. But this is nothing compared with milk, which has a polluting power of over 1,000 units.

THE DEADLY CHAIN

Chemicals known as PCBs, or polychlorinated biphenyls, are found in lubricants, hydraulic systems, cement, adhesives, and plastics. They are also found in lakes, such as Lake Michigan, near industry. They get there in effluent from factories and in polluted air from factory chimneys.

PCBs are picked up by plankton as they filter the water for food. They are passed on to the small fish that eat the plankton and then to larger fish. At each stage in the food chain, PCBs become more and more concentrated. Fish in the lake often have liver damage and grotesque skin tumors (cancers). People who eat fish caught in Lake Michigan have been found to have much higher levels of PCBs in their blood than people who do not eat fish. But no one is sure whether this is directly linked to cancers in humans. It may be too soon to tell, as cancers often take a long time to develop. In the meantime, many people think it sensible not to eat Lake Michigan fish.

▲ Litter is piled up by the wind at one end of this marina on Lake Michigan. But bigger dangers may lie in the lake itself.

KILLING FIELDS

Pollutants can also act more directly, as poisons. Agricultural chemicals used for killing weeds or animal pests can also be washed into nearby waterways. Since they are designed to kill plants and animals on land, they can do it in water, too.

◀ Children playing on a beach in Romania. Industry is vital to the economy, but as in many Eastern European countries industrial pollution is a huge problem in Romania.

▶ The original statue of the Roman goddess Ceres, which stood in central Copenhagen, Denmark, was damaged beyond repair by air pollution. This replica has been made to replace it.

HOW POLLUTION OCCURS

We have already seen that water pollution can occur when waste or other polluting materials are washed in from the surrounding land. But pollution of water can come from many sources and can occur at all stages in the water cycle.

ACID IN THE AIR

Acid rain is caused mainly by sulfur and nitrogen oxides from the burning of fossil fuels, such as coal and oil in power stations, motor vehicles, and industry. These gases mix with water vapor, sunlight, and oxygen in the atmosphere to form dilute sulfuric and nitric acid. These acid droplets may be transported hundreds or even thousands of miles (kilometers) to fall as acid rain, snow, or even dry particles.

A MOVING PROBLEM

Nearly a quarter of Sweden's lakes are affected by acid rain. Many of them no longer have fish living in them—some have no life at all. Thousands of lakes in the eastern United States and in Ontario, Canada, have acid levels at which most fish die.

Although some improvements have been made in Europe and North America, the problem is growing elsewhere. China is now the world's third-largest producer of sulfur dioxide, and acid-rain damage is spreading to other rapidly developing countries like India, Nigeria, Colombia, Venezuela, and Brazil.

► Pollution of the world's seas and rivers

Acids are not the only problem. PCBs and other dangerous chemicals, such as dieldrin, which is used in pesticides, also travel by air. Lake Superior—one of the Great Lakes in North America—gets 80 percent of its pollution this way.

▼ Industry in the city of Shanghai, China, brings much-needed wealth to the country—but at what cost?

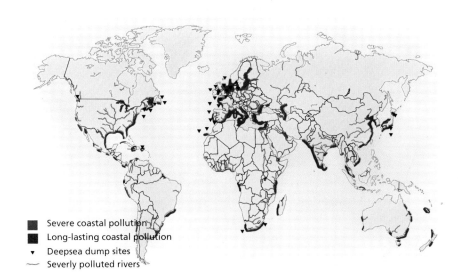

■ Severe coastal pollution
■ Long-lasting coastal pollution
▼ Deepsea dump sites
~ Severly polluted rivers

POLLUTING THE SEAS

Many types of pollution that affect rivers and lakes, such as organic pollution and heavy metals, also affect the sea. Traces of DDT (an insecticide) and PCBs have been found in Arctic seals and Antarctic penguins, and in rat-tail fish dredged up from 10,000 ft. (3,000 m). Many countries still use the sea to dump toxic chemicals, sewage sludge, and garbage from their cities. Two-thirds of the sewage pumped into the Mediterranean Sea has had little or no treatment. Seas surrounded by land, like the Black Sea and the Baltic Sea, are often the worst affected because there is less circulation of water and more coastline.

COUNTING THE COST

In March 1989, the hull of the oil tanker *Exxon Valdez* was ripped open on Bligh Reef in Prince William Sound, off the coast of Alaska. More than 50,000 tons of oil fountained from its tanks. Within a month the oil had traveled more than 120 mi. (200 km) along the coast. Thousands of seabirds and sea otters froze to death—their oil-soaked feathers and fur were not able to trap air and keep the animals warm.

29

WHY POLLUTION OCCURS

Pollution is not always caused by humans. For example, large quantities of leaves falling into a pond decompose and use up oxygen, causing fish to die. Certain types of phytoplankton in lakes or the sea can multiply rapidly, releasing toxic chemicals that may be fatal to other forms of life. But recovery from this kind of natural pollution is usually rapid. Pollution created by people is a different matter.

One reason pollution occurs is that we tend to treat water as a kind of bottomless garbage can. We think that we can dump our trash and waste in it and it will simply disappear.

GETTING THE BENEFITS— PAYING THE PRICE?

But perhaps the real reason water pollution occurs is that we often make unreasonable demands on our environment. For example, we expect to get the maximum amount of food from as little land as possible. We therefore use chemicals (fertilizers and pesticides) to improve crop yields and kill pests. We have already seen what happens when these get into watercourses. In the same way, we often concentrate farm animals in small areas, feeding them on artificial food and producing enormous quantities of animal waste. It isn't hard to imagine what happens when this waste escapes into rivers.

LOST AT SEA

Every year, 150,000 tons of plastic fishing nets and line are dumped or lost in the sea, and countless plastic containers are thrown overboard from ships. Plastic does not break down easily. Nets floating in the water are almost impossible to detect, and each year a million seabirds and 100,000 marine mammals die as a result of becoming entangled in, or swallowing, what we call litter.

Water taken from the Po River irrigates these crops in central Italy, making this area one of the most fertile in the world. But as more and more water is removed, the river itself is threatened.

Our demand for manufactured and luxury goods means that we rely heavily on industry, with its high consumption of energy and use of complex chemical processes. Again, the result is that we put more and more pressure on our water supplies. Meanwhile, in the developing countries, poverty and lack of infrastructure—basic equipment and conveniences—often result in contaminated water and inefficient, polluting industries. As these countries develop further, these problems are likely to grow.

We get the benefits of what is called development, but are we prepared to pay the price in terms of a damaged environment? How can we reduce the damage without necessarily forfeiting our standard of living? And how can developing countries gain the benefits we have achieved without putting an unbearable burden on water supplies and the environment generally? These difficult questions are examined on pages 34–44.

▲ Rainwater washes out pollution from this mine dump in Colorado. Manufactured goods need raw materials, but their extraction can have damaging effects on water supplies.

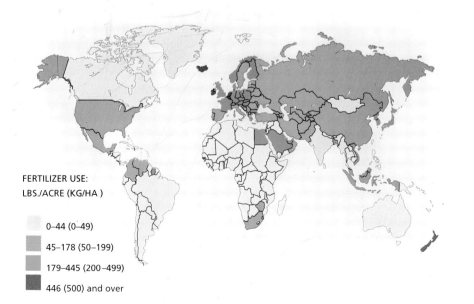

FERTILIZER USE:
LBS./ACRE (KG/HA)

0–44 (0–49)

45–178 (50–199)

179–445 (200–499)

446 (500) and over

◀ Worldwide use of fertilizers: Artificial fertilizers can improve crop yields dramatically, but their widespread use can damage the soil and pollute nearby water supplies.

SHORT OF WATER

Each year, enough rain falls throughout the world to cover all the continents with a layer of water 32 in. (81 cm) deep —more than enough for all our needs. But rain does not fall evenly, and the world's population is divided into those people who have enough water and those who do not.

HAVES AND HAVE-NOTS

Iceland gets sufficient rain and snow to provide its people with enough fresh water every year to fill over 600 Olympic-sized swimming pools per person. In Israel and Saudi Arabia, 3,000 people have to share the same amount, but in neighboring Kuwait there is hardly more than a bucketful of rain for each person.

Changes in global climate—global warming—could make the situation worse. Some scientists predict that the entire western United States will lose half its present rainfall within the next 50 years. Growing human and animal populations will put greater pressure on existing water resources. By the year 2000, Egypt will only have two-thirds as much water for each of its people as it did in 1990, and Kenya will have only half as much.

▼ Water supply worldwide: Although there is enough water for everyone on the planet, its uneven distribution means that many people have insufficient even to meet basic needs.

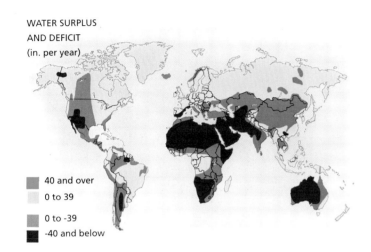

WATER SURPLUS
AND DEFICIT
(in. per year)

- 40 and over
- 0 to 39
- 0 to -39
- -40 and below

▼ The long trek: the job of carrying water often falls on women, and the task can take up most of the day. This means that there are few opportunities for education or relaxation.

AN UPHILL STRUGGLE

The village of Adi Baren, southern Ethiopia, is almost 4 mi. (6 km) away from the nearest source of water. Gue'y Baryagbar came to the village when she was nine. She had to carry a heavy pot to the river and then return with it full— a load weighing over 60 lbs. (27 kg)—walking up steep, rocky paths. Often she fell, injuring herself and smashing the pots. That was 40 years ago. She still makes the same journey every day.

A RIVER DRAINED DRY

The Colorado River rises in the Rocky Mountains of North America. By the time it reaches the Pacific Ocean it has supplied 21 million people, watered 1.2 million acres (0.5 million ha) of farmland, and replaced rapidly falling groundwater. For 2,000 years, the Cucapa Indians have lived in the river's delta by the Gulf of California, planting vegetables after the floods and eating fish three times a day. Now the delta is filled with weeds, trash, and stagnant swamps. The Cucapa are lucky to eat fish once a week. "We are the river people," says Ricardo Sandoval. "But what river? I haven't seen it. It doesn't get this far."

GOING UNDER

When there is not enough rainwater, people turn to the vast quantities of water trapped underground. But, like rainfall, it is unevenly distributed and often difficult to get at. Under the Great Plains of the United States lies a huge aquifer that extends across eight states. Yet the level of water is falling by up to 3 ft. (1 m) a year as more and more water is taken to water crops, power industry, and supply towns and cities. Beneath the city of Bangkok in Thailand, the water table has fallen 80 ft. (24 m), allowing saltwater to flow into wells. As water is removed, the ground is gradually sinking, taking the city with it.

▲ This irrigation canal snaking through the California desert drains water from the Colorado River. Water levels in the river are now seriously threatened.

▼ As underground water is removed to supply the growing city of Bangkok, the land is subsiding. Now the city, too, is slowly sinking.

WHAT CAN BE DONE?

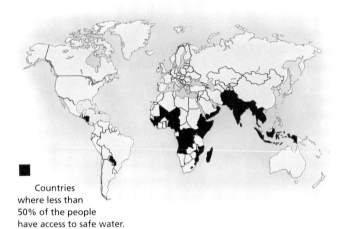

▼ Areas of the world where most people do not have access to safe water supplies.

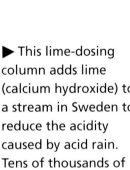

Countries where less than 50% of the people have access to safe water.

It would be easy to be gloomy about the future of our water supplies, especially from a worldwide viewpoint. But there is much that is being done already—and that can be done in the future—to make clean water a basic right for everyone.

DOES MORE MONEY MAKE CLEANER WATER?

In 1980, the United Nations launched a 10-year water program. Its aim was "clean water and adequate sanitation for all by the year 1990." India and some other countries increased their funding for water projects six times over, and foreign aid from the richer countries was increased. Hundreds of millions of people were given safe water and proper sanitation for the first time.

▶ This lime-dosing column adds lime (calcium hydroxide) to a stream in Sweden to reduce the acidity caused by acid rain. Tens of thousands of similar columns would be needed to have a widespread effect.

But there were problems. Pumps broke down; new wells were not maintained; and latrines fell into disrepair. As a result of these factors—together with increases in the world population, civil wars, and droughts—the same number of people are still at risk today from dirty water as were in 1980.

SAVING THE SEAS

The sea is no longer an automatic dumping ground. Radioactive waste dumping was stopped in 1983, and the dumping of industrial wastes and sewage sludge is being scaled down. So is the burning of toxic waste at sea. Oil tankers are no longer supposed to wash out their tanks at sea, although many still do when they are out of sight.

Since the sea has no borders, countries are now working together to protect it. All the nations surrounding the Baltic are cooperating to save the sea, the deeper parts of which now contain no living things. Now the developed countries are taking pollution seriously, but they still have a long way to go.

CLEANING UP THE AIR

Acid lakes can be neutralized and brought back to life by adding powdered lime. But this is expensive and does not tackle the real cause. Tougher laws on air pollution are the only real answer. Most countries in the EU (European Union) should have cut their emissions of sulfur dioxide by 40 percent by the year 1998 and by 60 percent by 2003. Since 1993 all new cars produced in Europe have been fitted with catalytic converters, which cut out acidic gases like nitrogen dioxide. The United States has tougher laws, but it also has more industry and more cars.

STICKING TO THE LAW

In the developed countries, laws regulate the amount of waste material that can be discharged into rivers or the sea. Industries, and water companies themselves, are fined if they go beyond these limits. But fines may not always be enough to prevent pollution from occurring—or to stop accidents. And even where laws exist, some countries simply cannot afford to make them work.

In wealthy Florida, water runoff from car-clogged city streets is responsible for 85 percent of the heavy metals found in the state's rivers and swamps.

▼ Sulfur dioxide pollution levels in some of the world's industrial cities.

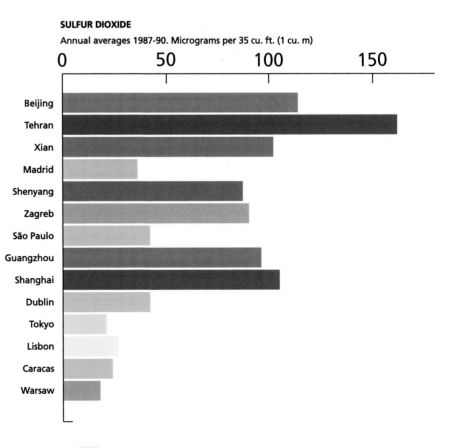

SULFUR DIOXIDE
Annual averages 1987-90. Micrograms per 35 cu. ft. (1 cu. m)

WHEN THE TIGERS AWAKE

While the developed countries seek to control their pollution, many of the developing countries are just beginning to set out on the road to full industrialization. Countries like Brazil, India, Korea, Taiwan, and China are developing powerful economies. They now challenge Europe and the United States in the production of manufactured goods, from cars to computers. Many of the countries of eastern Asia are known as "tiger economies" waiting to spring into action as their industries develop.

These workers in Malaysia are being trained to deal with a chemical spillage. But industries should try to make sure that such accidents do not take place at all.

What will be the effect on the health of the world's water supplies when these sleeping tigers awake? At present, the signs do not look good. Many of India's rivers have been described as little more than open sewers. More than 300 mi. (483 km) of the Ganges River is polluted with industrial and human waste. Many of Malaysia's rivers have been dangerously polluted with human and animal waste and with increasing amounts of toxic wastes from industry. Only a tenth of the factories pumping waste directly into those rivers have treatment plants. In China 54 out of 78 of the main rivers are seriously damaged by waste from rubber processing and oil palm manufacturing.

Many of the poorer developed countries too—such as those of Eastern Europe and Russia—have industries that are poorly equipped and poorly controlled. Pollution from the Vistula River in Poland can be followed for 180 mi. (290 km) across the Baltic Sea until it arrives in Sweden.

WHO IS TO BLAME?

Can we blame the developing countries for following the same pattern that the developed world took in the past? Now that we have benefited from our development, can we criticize those who want to follow? The developed countries have both the technology and the wealth (in many cases earned at the expense of developing countries) to tackle their pollution problems. The developing countries have neither.

If there is an answer it must surely be that the developed nations of the world have to share both their technology and wealth to ensure that the new industrial countries do not also become the new polluters. We now understand more about the causes of water pollution and how to prevent it. It is in everyone's interests for clean water to be available as a global resource.

The question for us all is: Are we prepared to invest in clean water across the globe, or do we close our eyes to what is happening elsewhere? If the answer seems obvious, the next question might be: To what extent would you be prepared to change the way you live in order to pay for it?

This waterworks in Bonfora City, Burkina Faso, will give more people access to clean, safe water. But technology like this is expensive for poor countries.

FINDING MORE OR USING LESS

The answer to the world water shortage seems less complicated than the problems of keeping it clean. We should either find more water or use less. In reality, the answers are much more difficult.

We use only about 3 percent of the rain that falls on land. About two-thirds of it evaporates straight back into the atmosphere, the rest flows into rivers and the sea or into the ground. Dams built across river valleys trap water and can generate electricity. But large dams often create new problems. They permanently flood large areas of useful land above the dam, and they interrupt the natural flooding of the fertile plains below it. The land around the Nile River in Egypt was once the most fertile in the world. Since the completion of the massive Aswan Dam in 1971, farmers have had to use artificial fertilizers, which are costly and less efficient. The fertilizers themselves can create pollution, so one set of problems has been swapped for another.

The Uribante Caparo hydro-electric dam project in Venezuela will bring benefits to many people, but there is also a price to pay in lost land and disturbance to the natural environment.

DOING MORE WITH LESS

We use water inefficiently. Of all the water used on crops, two-thirds gets wasted. Cutting waste along the Indus River by only 10 percent would solve many of Pakistan's water shortage problems. Improving the flow of water along irrigation channels and using sprinklers that deliver water straight to crop roots can cut wastage by 80 percent. Such methods are used in the United States, Commonwealth of Independent States, France, and Italy but are still not widespread. Other countries such as Israel are using wastewater to irrigate crops.

The recycling of water—re-using it several times before it is discarded and treated—is becoming more common. Israel recycles nearly half of its water and plans to recycle four-fifths by the year 2000. It has also cut its use of water in industry by 70 percent. Factories in the United States use water up to three times before getting rid of it.

Perhaps for the first time, many people in the richer countries are beginning to experience real water shortages. These shortages may not threaten our lives—but they may help us to realize that we need to manage our resources more carefully than ever before.

At this hotel in Bangkok, Thailand, wastewater is being recycled to water the gardens.

DROUGHT BUSTERS

Tucson, Arizona, is a desert city that thrives on little water. Its streets and parks are planted with trees and shrubs that grow naturally in the surrounding Sonoran Desert. Local bylaws state that "low-flow" faucets, showers, and toilets must be installed. Golf courses and parks are watered with treated sewage effluent. And the streets are patrolled by city "drought busters" looking for signs of waste—a sort of water equivalent to traffic cops.

Even so, Tucson's water has to come from somewhere. It has been suggested that although the city has a good record of saving water, Tucson is gradually draining water from the aquifer beneath a neighboring Navajo reservation.

INVOLVING PEOPLE

Here are four short stories about people and water. All of them are true. The first three illustrate the work of WaterAid, a charity that helps people to build and maintain their own water supplies.

PEOPLE POWER

In the Hitosa region of southern Ethiopia, hundreds of volunteers work on one of the largest water projects in the country. Every day Sulti Tulo walks two miles (3 km) from his village to help dig the trench for the main pipeline. "Because of the lack of water there were sanitation problems—so each day I bring over 60 people from the village to work on the pipeline. Sometimes I bring 200 people to help." When it is complete, the gravity-fed project will supply safe water to 63,000 people in 28 villages and three towns.

▲ Sulti Tulo and his fellow villagers work on a pipeline that will bring clean water to many local villages and towns.

WATER FOR CHANGE

In Chainpur in Nepal, safe water is within three minutes' walk of each home. Most of the houses have their own private latrines. Both are the results of the village water committee, which worked with Nepal Water for Health to build new wells and start education programs about hygiene. Since the project has been running, the villagers' health has improved dramatically. Children suffer less from water-borne illnesses like diarrhea and dysentery. Diets have improved because vegetables can be grown nearby. "All the women in the community now have time to attend literacy classes," says Radhika Khadka, one of the women on the water committee. "Now that we have safe water, we are looking for simple industry for the village, like knitting and sewing, so the women can earn money."

◀ A class in Chaimpur, Nepal, to tell people about water cleanliness. Learning about hygiene makes people more aware of practices that contaminate their water supplies.

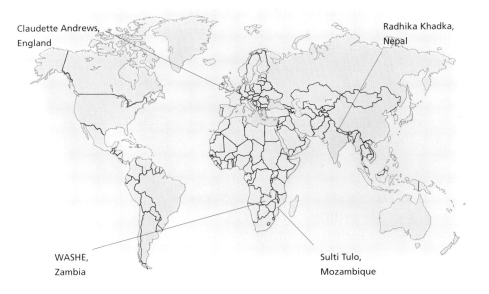

Claudette Andrews, England

Radhika Khadka, Nepal

WASHE, Zambia

Sulti Tulo, Mozambique

◄ This map shows the locations of the four stories featured on these pages.

▼ Learning by doing: Demonstration wells like this one in Zambia show people what can be achieved.

SPREADING THE WORD

In Monze, Zambia, the Water, Sanitation, and Health Education committee (WASHE) is working with WaterAid. WASHE has trained local Environmental Health Technicians (EHTs) in well construction, pump maintenance, and education. Now the EHTs help local communities improve their water supplies and sanitation. Over the next three years, WASHE plans to encourage the building of 180 wells and 1,200 latrines, training 360 village health education workers, and setting up 180 water committees.

VALUING WATER

Claudette Andrews is an education officer working for Thames Water in the south of England. Her job is to talk to teachers, students, and young people about water. She wants to show people that water is an important resource that should be valued, no matter where you live. "Once people realize that the water they use now could one day be washing an Ethiopian baby or rushing down the Colorado River, they start to appreciate how important it is to use it wisely," she says. "It's not our water, or somebody else's water—it's everyone's; so we all have a responsibility to look after it."

▼ Claudette Andrews at work in a school

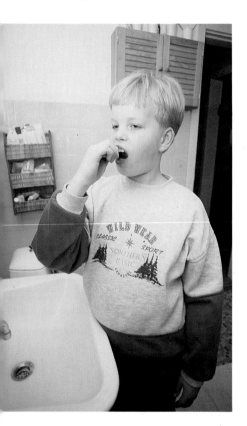

▼ Every little bit helps: by making sure the faucet is turned off while cleaning his teeth, Kasper from Denmark is helping to safeguard water supplies.

TAKING RESPONSIBILITY

If you think there is very little that you can do to protect water supplies, think again. Here are some ways you too can help the water cycle do its job.

SAVING WATER

Saving water is perhaps the easiest thing to do. There are lots of ways in which it is possible to cut down how much we use:

DON'TS

- Try to avoid using more water than you have to. For example, when you are brushing your teeth, don't leave the faucet running. That could save more than one gallon (5 l).
- When you have a bath, don't run too much water. A deep bath can hold more than 26 gallons (100 l) of water.

DOS

- Take a shower—if you have one—rather than a bath. A short shower uses up about a third as much water as an average bath.
- Make sure faucets are turned off fully. Even a slowly dripping faucet can waste 3 gal. (11 l) a day, and a faucet left running can waste 2,600 gal. (9,800 l) a day.
- Have a look at the cistern that flushes the toilet. If it's a fairly old one, the chances are it uses more water than it needs to— less than 2 gal. (7.5 l). It's possible to get a special device to put in the cistern to take up some of the space. (Don't use half a brick—the toilet may not flush properly.)
- Every time you use water, ask yourself two questions: Is it necessary? Can I do it with less? Try to figure out what you use normally and how much you could save in a week.

▶ Getting involved: These adults and young people are helping to maintain the flow of this shallow river by clearing out trash and mud.

Schools use massive amounts of water. A school of, say, 600 pupils can use more than 1.9 million gal. (7 million l) a year. Many of the ways that schools can reduce their use of water and help keep it clean are the same as those at home. The difference is that when people work together, it's often possible to do more.

KEEPING IT CLEAN

It is just as important to reduce or stop doing things that can pollute water.

DON'TS

● Don't use too much detergent or dishwashing liquid even if they are environmentally friendly; the water still has to be treated to some extent at a treatment plant.

● Never pour oil, paint, or any other chemical down the drain or toilet. Most local authorities provide facilities for the safe disposal of harmful chemicals, at the local dump site.

● Try not to use ordinary bleach or other strong disinfectant unless it is really necessary; if something kills a whole range of household germs, it probably kills everything else as well. There are friendlier alternatives.

● Don't leave litter around, especially plastic litter or fishing line and hooks.

DOS

● Use cleaning or cosmetic products that are environmentally (and animal) friendly. Don't believe everything you read on the label, though. If you're not sure, call the manufacturer or get in touch with an environmental organization to find out if you can safely use something.

● Keep an eye out for signs of water pollution. These could be dead fish, strange smelling or discolored water, or someone emptying a load of waste into the local stream. If you suspect anything, contact the water company or local authority.

● Where possible, encourage the person in your household who buys food to buy meats or vegetables that have been grown organically. This means that artificial chemicals have not been used in their production. Unfortunately, organic produce is usually more expensive than nonorganic.

This mechanic is collecting old oil from cars so that it can be recycled. If it were poured down a drain, it could pollute nearby rivers and lakes or even the sea.

WATER FOR THE FUTURE

In June 1992, leaders of over 150 countries met in Rio de Janeiro, Brazil, to take part in the largest environmental conference ever held; it became known as the Earth Summit. The leaders and environmental experts talked about the need for sustainable development—that is, how we can provide for the needs of the present without damaging the resources on which future generations will depend. One of those resources is water.

FOR RICHER OR POORER?

We have seen that the earth has a finite amount of water and that this is constantly being recycled naturally between the sea and the land, lakes and rivers, plants and animals.

Although water is practically impossible to destroy, it is easily damaged or polluted. When this occurs, people and all living things that depend on water are also harmed. This book has shown how people's actions have created water shortages and damaged supplies. It has also shown that this occurs in both rich, developed countries and poor, developing countries.

▲ These Danish children take it for granted that the water is clean. But we have to make sure that water will still be safe for future generations.

▼ U.S. vice-president Al Gore makes a point at the Earth Summit in Rio in 1992.

The way people in the richer countries live tends to be based on using very large amounts of water, all of the very highest quality, in our homes and in industry. At the same time, we demand goods and manufactured products that encourage the use of complex, often dangerous and long-lived chemicals that are released into the environment. Our demand for large quantities of food, grown in perfect condition on limited amounts of land, has encouraged intensive farming methods. These require the use of agricultural chemicals that have also endangered our water supplies. We have also seen that many of the world's water problems now rest with the poorer, developing countries. How we work together to solve these problems is one of the biggest issues we will ever face.

Meanwhile, people in the developing world are demanding what we in developed countries have grown used to—greater wealth, plentiful food, and lots of manufactured goods and services to choose from. The farmers, industrialists, and businesspeople in those countries are going all out to satisfy these demands, with little concern for the environmental costs. As a result, water pollution is now increasing dramatically in developing countries.

▲ A group of Nigerian boys in the lake created by a waterfall. Clean water should be a right for all people in all the countries of the world.

TIME TO CHANGE

We need to start looking at water in a new way: not as an inexhaustible supply or a convenient dumping ground; not as something we think about only when we get brown water out of the faucet or hear about a drought on the news. Water is something that affects almost everything we do, and, along with the air we breathe and the food we eat, it keeps us alive.

ALL TOGETHER NOW

This book has mentioned ways in which communities and individuals can help improve water supplies. But little can be achieved unless governments and other organizations also work together. The only way that real progress can be made is if we consider water in all its forms—in the sea, in the atmosphere, and on land—and the connections between them. Water does not recognize boundaries, so we too need international cooperation and planning in order to safeguard water supplies now and for the future. That was what the Earth Summit tried to achieve.

GLOSSARY

AQUIFER An underground water supply, where water is held within porous rock, rather like a sponge.

BOREHOLE A deep well, usually drilled through rock, to obtain water from an aquifer.

DEVELOPED COUNTRIES Well-off countries, mostly in the Northern Hemisphere, with highly developed industries and services such as roads, hospitals, water supplies, schools, etc., but also often having problems such as high crime rates, pollution, road accidents, and diseases associated with overeating, smoking, etc.

DEVELOPING COUNTRIES Often poor countries, mostly in the Southern Hemisphere, which are largely agricultural and in which services like schools, proper sanitation, and hospitals may not be well developed.

DORMANT Undisturbed or inactive.

EFFLUENT Water coming out of a factory or wastewater treatment plant.

EVAPORATION The process by which a liquid becomes a gas, such as water vapor.

FERTILIZER Natural or artificial substances that provide extra nutrients to plants.

FOOD CHAIN The way animals and plants are connected by feeding relationships; usually more correctly called a food web since it has many strands and interconnections.

FOSSIL FUELS Fuels such as coal, oil, and gas that are formed from the fossilized remains of plants.

HEAVY METALS Metals with a high atomic mass such as mercury, lead, and cadmium, often used in industry but highly poisonous.

INCINERATE To destroy by burning.

INTENSIVE FARMING Growing crops or raising farm animals in a limited space and often requiring the addition of large quantities of agricultural chemicals and animal feeds.

MARINE Having to do with the sea.

MIGRATIONS Regular journeys undertaken by animals or people, usually to find better conditions at different times of year.

NUTRIENTS Simple chemicals in solution (dissolved) in water, such as nitrates and phosphates, used by plants in order to grow.

ORGANIC WASTE Waste made of either plant or animal matter.

ORGANOCHLORINES Complicated, manufactured chemicals containing hydrogen, oxygen, carbon, and chlorine and used for a wide variety of purposes but which are damaging to the environment.

PARASITE An animal that spends at least part of its life inside or on another animal, usually obtaining food from it.

PHYTOPLANKTON Microscopic plants (algae) floating in the sea and large lakes.

POLLUTION The result of harmful materials being released at a greater rate than they can be coped with by the environment.

PREDATOR Any animal that kills and eats other animals.

RESERVOIR A natural or artificially created body of water used for generating power and/or providing water supplies.

SANITATION Any process by which water used by humans is treated so that it can be returned safely to the environment.

SUSTAINABLE DEVELOPMENT Ways in which a country can develop or improve conditions for its people without threatening the resources, such as land and water, on which the country depends.

TEMPERATE CLIMATE Climate with warm summers and cool winters; usually situated between the tropics and the polar regions.

WASTEWATER Water after it has been used by people or industry and which must be treated (made cleaner) before it can be allowed back into rivers or the sea.

WATER MAIN Part of a network of pipes that distribute water to houses, industry, etc.

ZOOPLANKTON Tiny animals floating in seas and lakes and feeding on phytoplankton.

FURTHER INFORMATION

ADDRESSES TO WRITE TO

The water companies that provide and treat water can be a very useful source of information. You can find your local water company in the Phone Book for your area.

Cetacean Society International
P.O. Box 953
Georgetown, CT 06829

Environmental Protection Agency
401 M Street, SW
Washington, D.C. 20460

Friends of the Earth
1025 Vermont Avenue, NW
Suite 300
Washington, D.C. 20005-6303
(202) 783-7400

International Marinelife Alliance
2800 4th Street North
Suite 123
St. Petersburg, FL 33704
(813) 896-8626

Office of Protected Resources
National Marine Fisheries Service
1315 East-West Highway, 13th Floor
Silver Spring, MD 20910

The Office of Water Resource Center
Mail Code (4100)
Room 261 S East Tower, Basement
Washington, D.C. 20460
(202) 260-7786

BOOKS TO READ

Anderson, Madelyn K. *Oil Spills.* (First Book.) Danbury, CT: Franklin Watts, 1990.

Baines, John. *Water.* (Resources.) Austin, TX: Raintree Steck-Vaughn, 1993.

Blashfield, Jean & Black, Wallace. *Oil Spills.* (Saving Planet Earth.) Danbury, CT: Children's Press, 1991.

Barss, Karen. *Clean Water.* (Earth at Risk.) New York: Chelsea House, 1992.

Christiansen, Peter. *Water.* (First Discovery.) New York: Scholastic, Inc., 1996.

Cossi, Olga. *Water Wars: The Fight to Control and Conserve Nature's Most Precious Resource.* Parsippany, NJ: Silver Burdett Press, 1993.

Gardner, Robert. *Experimenting With Water.* Danbury, CT: Franklin Watts, 1993.

Hoff, Mary & Rodgers, Mary M. *Our Endangered Planet: Groundwater.* Minneapolis, MN: Lerner Group, 1991.

—— *Our Endangered Planet: Rivers and Lakes.* Minneapolis, MN: Lerner Group, 1991.

Lampton, Christopher. *Drought.* (Disaster.) Ridgefield, CT: The Millbrook Press, 1992.

Lucas, Eileen. *Water: A Resource in Crisis.* Danbury, CT: Children's Press, 1991.

Morgan, Sally & Morgan, Adrian. *Water.* (Designs in Science.) New York: Facts on File, 1994.

Ocko, Stephanie. *Water: Almost Enough for Everyone.* New York: Atheneum Books, 1995.

Sauvain, Philip. *Water.* (Way it Works.) Parsippany, NJ: Silver Burdett Press, 1992.

Wekesser, Carol. *Water: Opposing Viewpoints.* San Diego: Greenhaven, 1994.

INDEX

Numbers that appear in **bold** refer to pictures as well as text.

acid rain 28, **34**–35
aquifers 14, 39
Australia 4

bacteria 9, 15, 20, 22–23, 26
Bangladesh **17**
boreholes 14
Brazil 28, 36, 44
Burkina Faso **37**

Canada 21, 28
catalytic converters 35
China **28**, 36
Colombia 28

dams 14, **38**
Denmark 7, **28**, **42**, **44**
diseases and illnesses 5, 24, **25**, 40
drought 35, 39, 45

Earth Summit (1992) **44**, 45
Ethiopia 32, **40**
Exxon Valdez **5**, 29

farming
    as cause of water pollution 5,
        26–27, 29–31, 38, 45
    use of water 11, 19, **30**, 33, 39
Finland 19

Germany 21–22
global warming 32
groundwater 6, **33**
Guatemala **22**

Iceland 32
India 22, **25**, 28, 34, 36

industry
    as source of water pollution 4,
        9, 11, 21, **27**, 28, 31, 36
    use of water 19, 33
Israel 32, 39
Italy **30**, 39

lakes **5**, 6–7, 10, 12–14, 23, 25,
        27–30, 35, 43–44
    Baikal **6**, 7
    Michigan **27**
    Superior 7
    Volta 25

Mozambique 41

Nepal 25, 40–41
Nigeria 28

ocean currents 12–13
oceans and seas 4–5, 7, 9–14,
        20–21, 29–30, 35–36, 38, 43–45
    Aral Sea 5
    Atlantic Ocean 12
    Baltic Sea 29, 35–36
    Mediterranean Sea 29
    Pacific Ocean 4, 7, 33

Pakistan 39
Poland 4, 36
pollution of water 4, **5**, 6–7, **9**, 11,
        12, **13**, 16, 21, **26**, 27–31, 35–38,
        43–45
    DDT 29
    dieldrin 29
    metals 21, **31**
    PCBs 27, 29
    sewage **13**, 20, **21**, **22**, **24**, 26,
        29, 35, 39
    trash 13, **22**, 29–30, 33, 42–43

reservoirs **14**, 15
rivers 4–7, 9–12, 14, 16, 20–22,
        25–26, 29–30, 32–33, 35–36,
        38–39, 41, **42**, 43–44
    Amazon 7
    Colorado 31, 33, 41
    Nile 7
Romania **27**
Russia 36

Saudi Arabia 32
Sweden 28, **34**, 36
Switzerland 11

Thailand 33, 39

wastewater
    recycling **39**
    treatment **19**, **20**, **21**, 22, **23**, 37

United Kingdom 4, 41
United States 4, 12, 27–28, **31**, 32,
        33, 35–36, 39, 44
    Alaska 5, 29
    Arizona 8, 19, 39
    Florida 35

vehicles and pollution 35–36, **43**
Venezuela 28, **38**

WaterAid 23, 40–41
wells 14, **16**, 17, 33, 35, 40, **41**
wildlife 6, 7, 9–13, 21, 26–27,
        29–30, 32, 36, 42–44

Zambia **41**

PICTURE ACKNOWLEDGMENTS

Environmental Images 14, 43 (Vanessa Miles); Forlaget Flachs 28 top (Schnakenburg and Brahl), 42 top (Ole Steen Hansen), 44 top (Hans Erik Rasmussen); Oxford Scientific Films 6–7 (Richard Kirby), 8 (Rodger Jackman), 19 top (Mike Birkhead); Panos 16 (Jim Holmes), 25 top (Magnus Rosshager), 26–7 (Sean Sprague), 33 bottom (Liba Taylor), 45 (Marcus Rose); Science Photo Library *cover background* (NASA), 23 (Prof David Hall), 24 (Argentum), 27 top (Van Bucher), 34 (Martin Bond); Still Pictures *front cover* (Mark Edwards), 5 top (Jean-Luc Zeigler), 12 (Andre Maslennikov), 13, 19 bottom (Mark Edwards), 20 (Herbert Giradet), 21 top (Bryan and Cherry Alexander), 21 bottom (Peter Frischmuth), 22 (Nigel Dickinson), 26 top (JP Vantighem), 28–9 (Max Fulcher), 30 (Mark Edwards), 37 (Jorgen Schytte), 39 (Mark Edwards), 44 bottom (Herbert Giradet); Thames Water Plc 41 bottom; Tony Stone Images 5 bottom (Alan Levenson), 9 (David Woodfall), 10 (Kevin Cullimore), 31 (David Hiser), 33 top (Mark Wagner), 38 (Simon Jauncey), 42 bottom (David Woodfall); WaterAid 4 (Jim Holmes), 17 (Jim Holmes), 25 bottom (Kelly Jones), 32 (Caroline Penn), 40 top (Caroline Penn), 40 bottom (Caroline Penn), 41 top (Tony Jones). Graphs and charts are by Tim Mayer. All other artwork is by Peter Bull, except the book icons used on page 2, the contents page and chapter headings, which are by Tina Barber.